Lamps of Fire

'Enfolded in Love' series
General Editor: Robert Llewelyn

LAMPS OF FIRE

Daily Readings with
St John of the Cross

Introduced, edited and illustrated by
Sister Elizabeth Ruth ODC

FOREWORD BY RUTH BURROWS

DARTON·LONGMAN + TODD

First published in 1985 by
Darton, Longman and Todd Ltd
1 Spencer Court
140–142 Wandsworth High Street
London SW18 4JJ

Reprinted 1987, 1995 and 1997

British Library Cataloguing in Publication Data

Elizabeth Ruth, *Sister*
  Lamps of fire: daily readings with St. John
  of the Cross
  1. Devotional calendars
  I. Title
  242′.2   BV4810

ISBN 0–232–51636–7

Phototypeset by Intype London
Printed in Great Britain by
Page Bros, Norwich

Contents

Contents

Foreword

St John of the Cross was one of those rare mortals who *lived* the truth that God is the meaning of human life. Our only fulfilment lies with him and the only life worth living is one lived in total conformity with his will; a practical, constant affirmation that God is the All-important. In his writings, in his direction, John strove to communicate his passion: how to reach divine union with all speed; how to attain an utterly selfless love for God and neighbour (the two are one) which is the highest contentment and joy. He is aware that his is no popular teaching but anyone who really wants God and not merely the enhancement of self in a 'spiritual life' will find satisfying nourishment in his 'substantial doctrine'.

The earnest heart rifling this treasury of texts selected for us by Sister Elizabeth, examining each with attention and eager to penetrate its God-filled meaning, will experience their power and unction. The prayer will surely rise up for a wholeheartedness of dedication hitherto unknown. 'O make up your mind', John is saying throughout, 'to give God all he asks.' If John's demands seem at times beyond the beyond we must ask ourselves if they exceed the demands of Jesus himself. Jesus is the criterion and the interpretative key to all John's asceticism:

Be continually careful and earnest in imitating Christ in everything, making your life conform

to his: for this end you must meditate thereon
. . . To do this well, every satisfaction offered
to the senses which is not for God's honour and
glory, must be renounced and rejected for the
love of Jesus Christ, who in this life had, and
sought, no other pleasure than doing the will
of his Father, which was his meat . . .

'. . . an instant of pure love is more precious in
the eyes of God and the soul, and more profitable
to the Church than all other good works together
. . .' For this can any price be too high?

RUTH BURROWS

Introduction

John of the Cross was born Juan de Yepes in Fontiveros, Castile, in the year 1542, son of a well-to-do father who had married a working woman and who, on account of his family's displeasure at this love match, had been disinherited. He therefore had to learn his wife's trade of weaving, and together they had struggled to make a living for themselves and their three sons. (Of the sons, one died in infancy, one was John, and then there was the eldest, Francisco, who was slightly mentally retarded.) John must have known in his early childhood the security of a home where love reigned despite material poverty. For it was love which pervaded all his writings, and it was love which made him, in his turn, a gentle and compassionate superior—a true father to those who lived under his authority. Even after both parents had died John retained all his life a genuine fondness for his elder brother, and was happy to have him near him whenever possible.

John's father died when he was about seven years old, and all responsibility fell on the hard-working mother, Catalina. She moved to Arévalo near Medina where she tried to apprentice John to several craftsmen. But he could find no stability until he was adopted by a retired businessman who had devoted himself to hospital work, and who, in return for practical help on the wards, provided John with a rudimentary education at a newly founded school run by the Jesuits.

As he came of age, John's thoughts turned to the religious life, and he entered the Carmelite Priory at Medina. He was then twenty years old.

It is to the Carmelite Order that we must look to understand much of John's spirituality. The Order originated in the twelfth century with a group of hermits, most probably former crusaders or pilgrims, who settled on Mount Carmel in Palestine. Naturally enough from their location they looked to the prophet Elijah as their model and inspiration, and considered themselves his spiritual heirs, attentive in solitude to the voice of God. However, as the Christians gradually lost control of the Holy Land the hermits migrated to Europe and, adapting themselves to prevailing conditions, established themselves as mendicant friars. This necessitated changes in the original Rule, and in many cases a decline in fervour. The 'roots' of the Order were always firmly planted in the tradition of the desert rather than in active work, but like many Orders they were by the late Middle Ages relaxed in discipline. On entering, John was given an education befitting one destined for the priesthood, and he studied at the University of Salamanca, one of the centres of Spanish theology, being ordained in 1567. It seems already he was longing for the more solitary life envisaged in the Rule and was considering transferring his allegiance to the Carthusians.

At this juncture of his life providence manifested itself in the person of that spirited woman, Teresa of Jesus, who herself had just founded a convent of reformed Carmelite nuns in Avila, and was hoping to persuade the men to follow suit. When she and John met in the autumn of 1567 she was fifty-two, he twenty-five. Immediately Teresa saw in him the material for inaugurating her project, and on his part John promised to defer his Carthusian aspirations if something could be arranged within the Carmelite Order for him and another friar, the elderly Antonio, prior of Medina del Campo. Teresa had 'a friar and a half' to begin the reform as she gaily remarked, joking about John's diminutive height. In fact, beside a woman of Teresa's physical vitality, charm and energy he seemed unprepossessing, but she divined the solid worth of his virtue, and together they became the great spiritual teachers not only of their own Order, but of Spain and the universal Church.

However, as often happens, the reform aroused jealousy. Without going into all the details of religious politics that unfortunately arise when ambition, envy and misplaced loyalty are allowed to rage unchecked, John was kidnapped by friars of the mitigated Rule and incarcerated in the prison of the Priory of Toledo. Here he was treated with great harshness, yet remained resolute in his chosen path. Publicly flogged, half-starved, humiliated, and physically almost at death's door, he learned to rely solely on God. And from this terrible prison he conceived the most sublime poetry of *The Spiritual Canticle*, that poem inspired by the Song of Songs, which sings of the soul's union with God the Bridegroom. At last, thanks to the aid of a friendly friar, John was able to escape one night letting himself down through a window by strips of sheeting. From there he hid in the Convent of the discalced (reformed) nuns of Toledo until the uproar died down. His experience is echoed in his masterpiece *The Dark Night of the Soul*:

> In a dark night
> With anxious love inflamed
> O happy lot!
> Forth unobserved I went
> My house being now at rest

After this episode John was free from molestation. He held various posts in the reformed Carmel—as master of students, prior, vicar-provincial and lastly as an ordinary friar. His friendship with St Teresa continued until her death. Another dear friend among the nuns was Anne of Jesus, Prioress of the Convent at Beas, for whom he most probably wrote his wonderful commentary on *The Spiritual Canticle*.

John was never a great leader in the normally accepted sense of the word, although he was instrumental in establishing several new houses of the Order, both for men and women. He had not the glowing charism of a St Teresa, but his personality was gracious, his interior life intense. As a contemplative he tried to make those with whom he came into contact share his ideals. There was nothing in him of the sour-faced, overly-penitential ascetic. All those with whom he lived testified to his gentleness in dealing with others, his deep compassion, yet his desire that all should attain to the union with God that he himself knew, and which demanded the total gift of self by firm and sustained inner discipline.

Now, as we know, human nature is such that those who strive for the highest are often misunderstood and belittled by those who make a 'career' out of religion. So with John. His last years were saddened by the tongues of scandalmongers and he was 'exiled' to the remote friary of La Peñuela, far from the centre of his Order's government, where he was free at last to enjoy his beloved solitude. But this interlude of peace was short lived. He fell ill with fever and in order to obtain medical aid was sent to Ubeda, where the prior showed towards the poor invalid an intense hostility. John, tender and loving as he had always shown himself towards the sick, perhaps as a result of his early hospital training, must have been wounded by this callous disregard, which only improved through the intervention of his friends. Here at Ubeda John grew gradually weaker until, on the evening of 14 December 1591, at the age of 49, he died, after listening to some verses being read from the Song of Songs. He who had loved so intensely went to enjoy forever the sight of the Beloved who had guided him to the heights of union even here on earth.

THE DOCTRINE OF JOHN OF THE CROSS

John of the Cross is known as the mystical doctor, because in a pre-eminent way he is the director of men on their interior journey towards God. As a spiritual guide and deeply religious man, trained in theology at the best Spanish universities of his day, he was able, as few others, to elucidate scripturally and doctrinally the ways of the Lord. Primarily, though, he is a poet, and his poetry speaks for itself in deeply symbolic language, the language of love. He is also a man of his country and era. His two poles Toda–Nada, All–Nothing, no doubt were associated for him with the rugged beauty of Castile—the blazing Spanish sky above arid ground, with the sun glinting upon walled cities, the freezing night with brigands concealed in the darkness. John and Spain speak the language of extremes, just as St Francis was a man of the Umbrian hills set with flowers and vines among shaded valleys. There is a tendency to contrast the harshness of one with the sweetness of the other, but this is to do a disservice to both. Both at heart are similar because they see the way to God as the way of giving all—desiring nothing but him, and letting the rest go: 'My God and my All'. In this, Jesus Christ is the model, and there is no spiritual growth apart from the earnest imitation of him. 'Be continually careful and earnest in imitating Christ in everything, making your life conform to his', John writes in *The Ascent of Mount Carmel*, almost as a key sentence. Only in this light can we understand his insistence on the denial of desires. What he has in mind are all those selfish and self-seeking ways we go about trying to have God and what we want as well. It is not that other people and other things are not lovable and desirable, or that God wants the way to him to be miserable. It is that the only *true* joy is found in Jesus, and having him we have all else besides.

John's writings sound demanding. He understood in an experiential way that God is not to be had on the cheap. Perhaps in our own day Bonhoeffer's works could be profitably re-read on the cost of discipleship, which John well knew—his had not been an easy life.

In the journey of the soul to God as John depicts it in the *Ascent* and the *Dark Night* he points to faith as the guide, and faith is dark to the understanding. We must just trust God and go forward with no assurance apart from his word. The saint probes the causes of why many begin this journey but make no progress. It is that self-love insinuates itself, and this must be eradicated by persistent effort in action and loving attention to God in humble prayer, no matter if we feel dry or empty of inspiration: John reveals the way of prayer as a way of great self-denial. We must not rely on anything we can see, feel, taste, experience, for God is more than all these. Only dark faith touches and holds him, and in this there is nothing to delight the senses or boost the ego.

By purifying the soul of all that is not God, God strips us in order to clothe us anew in Christ. Nothing gives place to the All, sorrow is turned into joy.

In *The Spiritual Canticle* and *The Living Flame of Love*, where John treats more explicitly of union with God, he does so in terms of lover and Beloved. In the former he bases his poem and commentary on the Song of Songs, in the latter upon the imagery of the Holy Spirit as flame, wounding and burning as it prepares the soul to be consumed in the fire of love's ecstasy.

But perhaps in his letters most of all we see

John as an understanding counsellor, warm and loving, yet allowing no compromises. The way of the Christian can only be the way of Christ and his cross, and John puts the Gospel demands before us in all their unadulterated strength. His is not a path of visions, ecstasies, abnormal phenomena. Rather, he rejects all these as diverting us from the God whom we can only know by faith, not by the 'spectacular' which many so-called spiritual people seek. Union is not felt bliss but 'the living death of the cross', as he says in the *Ascent*. God has spoken his final word in his Son, we have no need to seek anything but him as he is revealed to us in his life and teaching. To want other words, other revelations, is to seek self.

In a book of extracts from John's writings it is impossible to encompass the fullness of his doctrine, I can only refer the reader to his complete works. I have tried to choose passages which seem to me most helpful for daily Christian life, encouragement along the path of faith, and the joy of fulfilment in God which awaits those who persevere in seeking. 'Seek and you shall find, knock and it shall be opened to you.' The words of Jesus are as true today as they ever were. Those who want God and seek him single-mindedly will find him to their everlasting joy—as did St John of the Cross.

SISTER ELIZABETH RUTH ODC
Carmel of Our Lady of Walsingham
Norfolk

The Soul is Guided by Faith

In a dark night
With anxious love inflamed
O happy lot!
Forth unobserved I went
My house being now at rest.

In darkness and in safety
By the secret ladder, disguised,
O happy lot!
In darkness and concealment,
My house being now at rest.

On the road to union with God the night of faith shall guide me.

Faith tells us of things we have never seen, and cannot come to know by our natural senses.

The light of faith is like the light of the sun which blinds our eyes because its light is stronger than our powers of sight. So the light of faith transcends our comprehension.

God's Nurturing

It must be realized that usually, after conversion, the soul is spiritually nurtured and fondled by God as a little child is by its devoted mother, who warms it close to her breast, nourishes it with sweet milk and soft food, and carries and caresses it within the circle of her arms.

But as the child grows up the mother gradually ceases her caresses, sets the child down, and makes it walk on its own feet. This is in order that it may abandon the ways of childhood and direct itself to more important and substantial occupations.

The loving mother is like the grace of God, for as soon as the soul is newly awakened he treats it in the same way, giving it the breast of his tender love as if it were an infant.

But souls must realize their weakness in this state. They must take courage and desire to be brought into the night where the soul is strengthened and prepared for true love of God.

The Work the Soul Must Do

Those beginners who make progress do not rely on visible instruments. They do not burden themselves with them, nor do they seek to know more than is necessary for acting rightly. Their eyes are fixed on God, and their desire is to please him.

With great generosity they give up all they possess, spiritual and material, for their joy is to be poor out of love for God and their neighbour. They set their sights only upon true interior perfection which is to please God in everything, and themselves in nothing.

It is right that the soul, as far as it is able, should work to purify itself, that it may merit that God take it into his Divine care and heal it of those imperfections before which it is helpless.

For, after all the efforts of the soul, it cannot by its unaided labours make itself fitted for union with God in love. God must take it himself into his own hands and purify it in the dark fire.

The Night of Sense[1]

There are three tests to ascertain whether dryness in prayer is the result of God's purgation or of our own sins.

The first is when we find no comfort either in the things of God or in created things. For when God brings the soul into the dark night in order to wean it from sweetness and to purify its sensual desires, he does not allow it to find sweetness or comfort anywhere.

The second is that the memory is ordinarily centred on God with painful anxiety and carefulness. The spirit becomes strong, more vigilant and more careful lest there be any negligence in serving God.

The third sign is inability to meditate or make reflections, and to excite the imagination as before, despite all the efforts we may make. For God now begins to communicate himself, no longer through the channels of sense as formerly, but in pure spirit.

---

[1] John of the Cross is often referred to as the Doctor of the Dark Night. This is because, as John saw it, the path to God can only be a way of darkness. Nothing we see, feel or imagine can put us into contact with his infinity. Faith demands that we allow God to purge our senses and go by a way that is dark to human knowledge. The nights of sense and spirit are both aspects of this one refining process as God works on us at ever deeper and incomprehensible levels.

From Meditation to Contemplation

 It behoves those who find themselves in this condition to take courage and persevere in patience. Let them not be overly concerned about themselves, but put their trust in God who never forsakes those who seek him with a pure and upright heart.

Neither will he withhold from them all that is necessary for them on this road until he brings them to the clear and pure light of love which he will show them in that other dark night of the spirit, if they merit to enter it.

The conduct to be observed in the night of sense is this. They will do enough if they keep patience and persevere in prayer. All they have to do is to keep their soul free, unencumbered and at rest from all thoughts and all knowledge.

They must not be anxious about their meditation, being content simply with directing their attention lovingly towards God; and all this without anxiety or effort, or any desire to feel and taste his presence.

More of the Same

I do not mean to lay down a general rule for the cessation of meditation; that should occur when meditation is no longer feasible, and only then, when our Lord, either in the way of purgation and affliction, or of the most perfect contemplation, shall make it impossible.

At other times, and on other occasions, this help must be had recourse to, namely, meditation on the life and passion of Christ, which is the best means of purification and of patience and security on the road, and an admirable aid to the highest contemplation.

Contemplation is nothing else but a secret, peaceful, and loving infusion of God, which, if admitted, will set the soul on fire with the spirit of love.

God enlightens the soul, making it see not only its misery and meanness, but also his grandeur and majesty.

Thus out of this night springs first the knowledge of oneself, and on that, as a foundation, is built up the knowledge of God.

Denial of Desire

The journey of the ascent to God must be a perpetual struggle to make our desires cease, and the more earnest we are in this the sooner we shall reach the summit.

He who loves anything alongside God makes light of him, because he puts into the balance with God what is infinitely beneath him.

Without self-denial we shall make no progress towards perfection, nor in the knowledge of God and ourselves. We are not to rely on a clear intellect or natural talents, and then imagine that any affections or desires we indulge in will not blind us, and gradually bring about our decline.

In general, the reason why many souls have no love or inclination towards virtue is that they harbour affections and desires which are neither innocent nor directed wholly towards God.

He therefore who loves anything beside God renders his soul incapable of the divine union and transformation into God.

The people of Israel did not find the manna sweet above all else, although it was so in fact, because they would not limit their desires to it alone. The sweetness and nourishment of the manna was not perceived by them, not because it was lacking, but because they longed for other foods beside it.

Everything else then must be given up. The bread of angels is not given to, neither is it meant for, that palate which is satisfied with merely natural food.

If only spiritual people knew how they are losing the good things of the spirit because they will not raise their desires above trifles. If they would only forego these they would receive the sweetness of all things in the pure food of the spirit.

That soul which has no other aim than the perfect observance of the law of God and the carrying of the cross of Christ will be a true ark, containing the true manna which is God.

The Soul an Altar

In the state of union the soul is an altar upon which the sacrifice of praise and love is offered and where God dwells alone.

Under the old law, the altar of sacrifice was to be hollow within. It is the will of God that the soul should be empty of all created things, and thus become a fitting altar for the King of heaven.

He who wants to ascend the mount of perfection to build an altar upon which to offer the sacrifice of pure love, praise and adoration, must first fulfil the commandments of Jacob. He must cast away the strange gods of earthly affections and attachments. He must purify his desires, and he must change his garments. This last God will do for him if he observes the first two commands.

God will change old to new by infusing into the soul a new knowledge and a new love, so that all that is human in the soul may become divine.

Courage to Go On

How sad it is to see certain souls, like rich merchant ships, laden with good works, spiritual exercises, virtues and gifts of God which, because they cannot summon up courage to break with certain tastes, attachments or affections never reach the harbour of perfect union. Yet it would cost them but a single vigorous flight to break the thread that holds them.

It is a matter for real sorrow when God has given them strength to break other and stronger fetters, those of vanity and sin, that they neglect their own progress and the attainment of such great blessings because they will not detach themselves from trifles.

Not only do they not advance, they fall back. For it is well known that on the spiritual road not to go on overcoming self is to go backwards, and not to increase our gain is to lose.

As wood can never be transformed into fire if one necessary degree of heat is missing, so the soul that has even one imperfection can never be perfectly transformed in God.

The Way of Self-Denial

That you may have pleasure in everything
Seek your own pleasure in nothing.
That you may know everything
Seek to know nothing.
That you may possess all things
Seek to possess nothing.
That you may be everything
Seek to be nothing.

In detachment the spirit finds peace and rest because it covets nothing. Nothing wearies it by elation, nothing oppresses it by dejection. It stands in the centre of its own humility.

Desire to be empty and poor for Christ's sake. This state must be embraced with a perfect heart and you must really want it. If your heart is truly engaged in these efforts you shall speedily attain to great joy and consolation.

Be continually careful and earnest in imitating Christ in everything, making your life conform to his.

Reflecting God's Light

To be born of the Holy Spirit is to be like to God with no stain of imperfection.

If the sun's rays strike a window, but the window is stained and dirty, the sun cannot shine through in the same way it would have done if the window were clean and spotless. All depends, not on the sun, but on the window. If the latter were perfectly clear the sun's rays would transform it, letting it reflect the light, even though the window preserves its distinct identity.

The soul resembles this window. By resigning itself to God, removing from itself every spot and stain of attachment to creatures and keeping the will united to God, it becomes immediately enlightened and transformed into him.

There cannot be perfect transformation without perfect pureness.

That soul which does not attain to the degree of purity corresponding with the light and vocation it has received from God can never be wholly content and at peace.

True Spirituality

O that someone would teach us how to understand, practice and feel what is involved in the profound lesson of self-denial given by our Lord himself, so that religious people may see how different their conduct ought to be from that which many of them think to be right!

If we cling to anything whatever, whether it comes from God or the world, we are not journeying in detachment and self-denial. We shall certainly lose our way and never be able to ascend by the narrow path.

True spirituality seeks for bitterness rather than sweetness in God, inclines to suffering rather than to consolation.

It knows that this is to follow Christ and deny self, while the other course is perhaps nothing but seeking oneself in God, which is the very opposite of love.

Friendship with Christ

For beginners the way of God consists in one thing only—in knowing how to deny themselves earnestly, both inwardly and outwardly, giving themselves up to suffer for Christ's sake. That spirituality which wants to travel in sweetness and ease, shunning the following of Christ is, in my opinion, nothing worth. He is our light and example.

When the spiritual man has been brought to nothing, when his humility is perfect, then will take place the union of the soul with God. This consists not in spiritual refreshment, sweetness and fine sentiments but in the living death of the cross.

I see that Christ is but little known by those who consider themselves his friends. These, loving themselves so much, seek in him their own comfort and satisfaction, and not his sufferings and death out of love for him.

If we are determined to submit ourselves and to carry the cross, we shall find in it great refreshment.

Peaceful Listening

We must bring the memory into silence, that the Spirit alone may be heard, saying with the prophet: 'Speak, Lord, your servant is listening'. This is also the state of the bride, for the Bridegroom says of her, 'My sister, my spouse is a garden enclosed, a fountain sealed', so that nothing may enter within.

Let the soul, then, be 'enclosed' without anxiety. He who, when the doors were shut, entered bodily among his disciples and said 'Peace be with you' in an unexpected and inconceivable way, will enter spiritually into the soul when it keeps the door of its powers closed—that is, memory, understanding and will.

God will then himself fill the soul with his peace, turning it into a river of peace.

Be therefore earnest in prayer, and hope in detachment and emptiness. Your good will not be long in coming.

Freedom of Spirit

The person who is detached from creatures is not disturbed during prayer or otherwise, and so, without losing precious time, he easily acquires heavenly treasure. On the other hand, the covetous man runs hither and thither within the limits of the chain binding his heart. Despite all efforts he can scarcely free himself even for a moment from the bondage of his thoughts, which run constantly to the place where he has fixed his heart.

The spiritual man must keep in mind that there is nothing a man can truly rejoice in except serving God, promoting his honour and glory, and directing all things to this end.

When a man is purged of all attachment to things the judgement is left clear as the sky when the mists have dispersed. His joy is not dependent on creatures, for while his heart is set on none of them he possesses them all.

Clear Judgement

To endure all things with a calm and untroubled mind not only brings many blessings to the soul, but also enables us to have a clear judgement about them, and to take appropriate steps for their betterment.

In all the events of life, however untoward they may be, the wise man encourages us to rejoice instead of giving way to sadness. In so doing we will not lose the greater good, peace of mind in both prosperity and adversity.

That man attains to spiritual freedom, clearness of judgement, repose, tranquillity and peaceful confidence, together with true worship and obedience of the will when he represses all joy in passing things.

Man has greater joy and comfort in creatures if he detaches himself from them. Once the mind is purified from clinging to the outward aspect of things it is able to penetrate to their interior truth.

Loving Others Purely

 When our hearts are free from liking and judging people merely according to their natural gifts we are not held captive by external and changing charms. We are instead free to love people as they really are, and we can penetrate more easily to the core of their personality, their true goodness.

When we love in this way our love is selfless and pleasing to God.

The more this kind of love grows the more our love of God grows with it; and the deeper our love for him the more we shall love our neighbour for the principle of both is the same.

A great benefit of this way of loving people is that it fosters a large-hearted spirit, which is as necessary in God's service as is interior freedom. With it temptations against love are easily overcome, we are able to endure all things peacefully, and the virtues grow and flourish within us.

The Glory of God

There are many Christians who are virtuous men, and who do great things, but their virtues and good works are utterly useless in the matter of eternal life, because they seek themselves in them, and not solely the honour and glory of God.

The Christian must keep in mind that the value of his good works depends on the love which motivates him to perform them for God. Those works are most perfect when wrought in the most sincere love of God, and with the least regard to present or future self-interest, joy and sweetness, consolation and praise.

The heart therefore must not rest in the joy, comfort, delight and advantages which holy habits and good works bring with them. It must refer all to God, desiring only that God may rejoice in what is done in secret, and with God's honour and glory as its only motivation.

Thus all the strength of the will will be concentrated on God.

The Living Flame

O living flame of love
That wounds so tenderly
In my soul's deepest centre.
As you are no longer oppressive
Perfect your work in me if it is your will.
Break the web of this sweet encounter.

Before the divine fire enters the soul and becomes one with its depths, the Holy Spirit wounds it, destroying and consuming the imperfections of its evil habits.

The soul suffers greatly in this, for in this state of purification the flame does not burn brightly but in darkness, and if it gives any light at all it is only to show up and make the soul experience its own weaknesses and defects.

It is not a refreshing, peaceful fire, but a consuming and searching one that makes the soul grieve at the sight of itself. The soul perceives its own smallness in comparison with the immensity of the flame.

God is our Deepest Centre

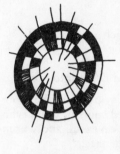

The centre of the soul is God. When the soul loves and understands and enjoys God to its utmost capacity it will have reached its deep centre, God.

Love unites the soul with God; and the more love the soul has the more powerfully it enters into God and is centred on him.

The soul which has one degree of love is clearly in its centre, God, since one degree is sufficient for it to abide in him through grace. If it has two degrees it enters into another more interior centre with God and so on. If it reaches the last degree, the love of God will be able to wound the soul at its deepest point; that is it is brought to the state where it appears to be God himself.

In this state the soul is like a crystal, limpid and pure. It is so enlightened it appears to be light itself.

God's Touch

O sweet burn!
O delectable wound!
O tender hand, O gentle touch
That savours of eternal life,
And pays the whole debt.
By slaying you have changed death into life.

O my God, the more gently you touch, the more
you are hidden in the purified souls of those who
have made themselves aliens on earth, and whom
you hide in the secret of your face.

O souls that seek your own ease and comfort! If
you only knew how necessary suffering is if you
are to reach union with God! If you understood
this you would take up the cross with the vinegar
and gall and account this a priceless favour,
knowing that by dying to the world and your
own selves you would then live for God in spiritual joy.

It is necessary for the soul to endure tribulations
with great patience, accepting all as coming from
God's hand for its healing and its good.

Water and Fire

O lamps of fire
In whose splendours
The deep caverns of sense
Dim and dark,
With a strange brightness
Give light and warmth together to the
  Beloved.

O wonder of wonders! The soul is inundated with the waters of the Divinity, which flow from God as from their abundant source.

When the soul offers the sacrifice of love it becomes living flames of fire. If we consider that the soul is transformed in God, it will be understood how, in some manner, it has in truth become a fountain of living water, boiling and burning in the fire of love—God himself.

Here the soul rejoices in the glory of God under the protection of his shadow. It is immersed in the waters of the Divinity which freely penetrate the whole person.

The Joy of God's Love

Whoever loves another does so according to his own attributes and properties. Therefore, since the Lord the Bridegroom is within you and is all powerful, he gives you power and loves you with the same.

Since he is wise he loves you with wisdom.
Since he is good he loves you with goodness.
Since he is holy he loves you with holiness.
Since he is just he loves you with justice.
Since he is merciful he loves you with mercy.
Since he is compassionate and understanding
  he loves you with gentleness and sweetness.

He loves you with the greatest humility and the deepest respect, making himself your equal and making you his equal. He joyfully reveals his face to you saying to you, 'I am yours, completely yours. And my happiness is to be who I am so that I may give myself to you and be all yours.'

God Speaks in Secret

 If a soul is seeking God, its Beloved is seeking it still more.

When the soul reflects that God is the guide of its blind self, then its main preoccupation will be to see that it sets no obstacle in the way of its guide, the Holy Spirit, upon the road by which God is leading it.

The soul then has to walk with loving advertence to God, without making specific acts, and exerting no effort on its own part. It must keep a simple, pure and loving awareness, like one who gazes with the awareness of love.

The soul must be attached to nothing, whether of sense or spirit, which would introduce noise into the deep silence. There the voice of God speaks to the heart in this secret place, in utmost peace and tranquillity.

God Carries the Soul

Wait upon God with loving and pure attentiveness, working no violence on yourself lest you disturb the soul's peace and tranquillity. God will feed your soul with heavenly food since you put no obstacle in his way.

The soul in this state must remember that if it is not conscious of making progress, it is making much more than when it was walking on foot, because God himself is bearing it in his arms. Although outwardly it is doing nothing, it is in reality doing more than if it were working, since God is doing the work within it. And it is not remarkable that the soul does not see this, for our senses cannot perceive that which God works in the soul.

Let the soul then leave itself in the hands of God and have confidence in him. Let it not trust itself to the hands and works of others, for if it stays in God's care it will certainly make progress.

Only God Gives True Light

There are two reasons for which the eye may not be able to see; either it may be in darkness or it may be blind. God is the light of the soul. If he does not illumine it, it is in darkness even if it has excellent powers of natural sight.

The light of grace which God gives to the soul, opening its eyes to behold the divine light, and making it pleasing to himself, calls to ever greater depths of grace, which will ultimately transform the soul in God.

If a man puts anything in his line of vision, however small, it is enough to obstruct his sight and prevent him from seeing other things in front of him; just so any small desire or idle act in the soul is sufficient to obstruct its vision of great and Divine things.

How impossible it is for a soul to judge the things of God aright! To do so it must completely get rid of its desires and pleasures apart from God.

God's Dwelling Place

How gently and lovingly
You awaken in my heart,
Where you dwell secretly and alone.
And in your sweet breathing
Filled with blessing and glory
You tenderly inspire me with love.

The dwelling of God is very different in different souls:

In some he dwells alone, in others not.
In some he dwells contented, in others displeased.
In some as in his own house, giving his orders
    and ruling it,
In others like a stranger in an alien dwelling.

Where personal desires and self-will are least in evidence, there he is most alone and contented. There he dwells as in his own house, ruling and directing it; and the more secretly he dwells the more he is alone.

O how happy the soul that is conscious of God reposing and resting within its breast!

Desire for God Alone

The waters of interior delights do not spring from the earth; the mouth of desire must be turned towards heaven, and be empty of everything else.

He then that seeks happiness in other things is not keeping himself empty for God to fill with his own unspeakable joy. As a man goes to God so does he leave him; and if his hands are full he cannot take into them what God wants to give.

Do not feed your spirit on anything apart from God. Cast away all cares and let peace and recollection fill your heart.

The soul that wants God to give himself to it wholly must first surrender itself totally to him, and keep nothing back for self.

God Takes Care of your Concerns

God takes care of the affairs of those who truly love him without their having to be anxious about them.

Let your soul cling to nothing, and if you continue to pray God will take care of your other concerns. This I find to be true of myself, for the more things I have, and the more I put my heart and soul into them, the more anxious I find myself over them.

O great God of love! How wonderfully you give your own riches to him who loves and takes pleasure in nothing apart from you. You give yourself to him and make him one with you through love. And you grant him to love and take pleasure in that which brings him the greatest gain.

For we must not be without our cross, even as our Beloved had his cross, until he died the death of love.

Advice on Disregarding Spiritual Sweetness

If a man is moved to love God apart from any sweetness he feels, he is already focusing his love upon God, whom he does not feel.

If he sets his will upon pleasurable and consoling feelings, thinking about them and resting in them, he is setting his will on creatures or related things, making them into an end instead of a means.

That man would be very ignorant who thinks that because sweetness and delight are failing him, God is failing him, or should think that in having these he is having God.

He would be still more ignorant if he followed God looking for sweetness, and rejoiced and rested in it when obtained. In this case his love is not set purely on God alone above all things, for in clinging to and desiring what is created, his will cannot soar to God.

Choosing God in All Circumstances

The more God gives the more he makes us desire, until we are empty and he is able to fill us with good things.

The immense benefits of God can only be contained by empty and solitary hearts. Therefore our Lord, who loves you greatly, wishes you to be quite alone, for he desires to be your only companion.

You must needs apply your mind to him alone, and in him alone content yourself, that in him you may find all consolation. Although God is always with us, if we set our hearts on other things beside him we cannot be at peace.

God knows what is best for all, and orders affairs for our good. Think on this only, that all is ordained by God. And pour in love where there is no love, and you will draw love out.

Rejoicing in Hope

The poor in spirit is more content and joyful when in want, for he has made nothingness his all, and found in it fullness and freedom of heart in everything.

O blessed is that nothingness, and blessed the secret depths of the heart that possesses everything. It desires to have nothing for itself, casting away all cares so that it may burn more brightly with love.

Live in faith and hope even though you are in darkness, for in this darkness God enfolds the soul. Cast your cares upon God, for you are his, and he will never forget you.

Read, pray, rejoice in God, your Good and your Health, and may he give you all good things and preserve you wholly—even to endless day.

Advice on Spiritual Progress

I desire your progress, but it strikes me that enough has already been said and written for the attainment of everything you need. If anything is lacking it is not writing or speaking (for generally there is a surfeit of these anyway), but silence and work.

Speaking distracts, whereas silence and work collect the powers and make us inwardly strong.

When a person has understood any helpful advice that has been given him, he does not need to hear or say more, but rather to put it into practice with silence and care, in loving humility and self-contempt.

He should not go seeking after new things which can only satisfy the desires in a superficial manner (and even here cannot satisfy fully) while leaving the spirit weak and empty, without deep inner virtue.

Suffering in Peace

 To preserve our spirituality there is no other way apart from silent suffering and labour, remaining faithful to the practice of solitude, and forgetfulness of all creatures and outward events even though the world should disintegrate about us.

Never fail to keep your heart at peace and in tender love, ready to suffer as things present themselves.

It is impossible to make progress except by working and suffering courageously, always in silence.

To have God in everything a soul must have nothing in everything, for how can a heart belong in any way to two people at once?

When anything disagreeable happens to you remember Christ crucified and keep silent.

Inward and Outward Silence

Keep yourself carefully from setting your thoughts upon what happens in the community, and still more from speaking of it except to the proper person and at the proper time. Nor should you ever be shocked or marvel at what you see or hear, but should try to keep your soul forgetful of it all.

For if you want to ponder on all that happens you would always discover something amiss even if you lived among angels.

Strive to keep your soul limpid and pure before God, undisturbed by thoughts of one thing or another.

Keep in mind what the apostle St James says: 'If any man thinks himself to be religious and does not control his tongue, that man's religion is useless.' This is to be understood of inward as well as outward chatter.

The Blessings of Spiritual Poverty

While you are walking in the dark and empty places of spiritual poverty, you think that everyone and everything is failing you. But that is hardly surprising, for it seems to you at such times that God is also failing you. But nothing is failing you, nor have you need to consult me about anything. All your anxiety is merely unfounded suspicion.

He who desires nothing but God does not walk in darkness, however blind and poor he may think himself to be. He that is not presumptuous, nor desires his own satisfaction has no need to falter or fret over anything. You are progressing well, remain in peace and joy. Who do you think you are to be anxious about yourself? You will only get yourself into a fine state!

You have never been in better dispositions than you are now, for you have never been so humble and docile, nor have you ever served God so purely and disinterestedly.

The Daily Round

What do you desire? What kind of life do you imagine yourself living in the world? How do you visualize yourself acting? What do you think the service of God involves if not abstaining from evil, keeping his commandments and doing his work as well as you can? When you do this what need is there to go seeking other instructions, other lights, other consolations, which usually conceal many snares and dangers for the soul which is easily led astray by its desires?

How can the soul walk aright and not wander from God's path except by following the highway of the laws of God and his Church, living in true and dark faith, with sure hope and perfect love, and dwelling here below as a pilgrim, exile and orphan, expecting everything from heaven?

Rejoice and put your trust in God for he has given you signs that you can, and indeed should, do so. He is leading you by a sure road. Do not wish for another way forward apart from this one. Establish your soul in peace, for all is well.

God in the Soul

God is hidden within the soul, and the true contemplative will seek him there in love.

O soul, most beautiful of creatures, who ardently longs to know the place where your Beloved is that you may seek him and be united to him. You yourself are the true tabernacle where he dwells, the secret room where he is hidden. Rejoice and exult, then, because all your good and all your hope is so near as to be within you. To speak more accurately you cannot be without him for 'the Kingdom of God is within you'.

What joy for the soul to learn that God never abandons it even in serious sin, how much less when it is in a state of grace.

Courage then, O soul most beautiful! You now know that your Beloved dwells hidden within your own breast. Endeavour therefore to be truly hidden with him.

The Beloved Bridegroom

God when loved readily listens to the prayer of the one who loves him. He says himself, 'If you live on in me, and my words live on in you, everything you ask for shall be yours.'

The soul may with truth call the Bridegroom Beloved when it is wholly his, when the heart has no attachments but him, and when all the thoughts are continually directed to him.

Some there are who call the Bridegroom their Beloved, but he is not really beloved because their heart is not wholly with him. Their prayers therefore are not so effective before God, and they shall not obtain what they ask until, by persevering in prayer, they fix their minds more constantly on God, and their hearts more wholly on him with loving affection; for nothing can be obtained from God but by love.

This is a test to discern the true lover of God. Is he satisfied with anything less than God? For the satisfaction of the heart is not found in possessions but in detachment from all things and poverty of spirit.

The Wounds of Love

Besides the many kinds of God's visits to the soul in which he wounds it with love, there are commonly certain secret touches of love which, like a fiery arrow, pierce and penetrate the soul, and burn it with the fire of love. These are properly called the wounds of love.

These wounds so inflame the will that the soul becomes enveloped with the fire of love. They make it go forth out of itself and be renewed, like the phoenix from the fire.

There can be no remedy for the wounds of love except from him who inflicted them, and so the wounded soul runs after the Beloved, crying to him for relief.

This spiritual running after God has a two-fold meaning. The first is a going forth from all created things. The second, a going forth out of oneself by self-forgetfulness; and this can only be accomplished by the love of God.

Resignation

O shepherds, you who go
Through the sheepcotes up the hill.
If you should see
Him whom I love
Tell him I languish, suffer and die.

The soul does no more than represent its miseries
and pain to the Beloved, for he who loves wisely
does not wish to ask for what he desires. He is
satisfied at hinting at his necessities so that the
Beloved may do what seems best to him.

There are three reasons for this. Firstly, our Lord
knows what is expedient for us better than we do
ourselves. Secondly, the Beloved is more
compassionate towards us when he sees our
necessities and our resignation. Thirdly, we are
more secure against self-love and self-seeking
when we represent our necessity instead of asking
for what we think we need. It is as if the soul
said, 'Tell my Beloved to save me, since I languish
and he is my salvation—that as I am suffering to
give me joy, since he alone is joy; that as I am
dying to give me life, since he alone is my life.'

The Seeking Soul

In search of my love
I will go over mountains and
strands.
I will gather no flowers,
I will fear no wild beasts,
And pass by the mighty and
the frontiers.

The soul, because its searching for the Beloved is real and its love great, will not leave undone anything it can do itself. The soul that really loves God is not easygoing in its efforts to find the Son of God, the Beloved. Even when it has done all it can it is still unsatisfied, feeling it has done nothing.

To find God we must work ourselves according to our capacity. The soul therefore, remembering the saying of the Beloved 'Seek and you shall find', is resolved to seek him actively and not rest until it finds him. For there are many who do not want God to cost them anything except empty words.

Seeking by Day

He who seeks God while attending to his own ease and comfort seeks him by night, and therefore does not find him. But he who seeks him in the practice of virtue and good works, disregarding comforts, seeks him by day. Such a one shall find him, for what is invisible at night can be seen by daylight.

The soul that leaves the house of its own will, and abandons the bed of its own satisfaction, will find the Divine Wisdom, the Son of God, the Bridegroom, waiting at the door without.

He that is resolved to seek God must have his heart detached and resolute, free from all evils and all goods which are not purely God.

The soul seems to say, 'I will not set my heart upon riches or the goods of this world; I will not indulge in the satisfaction of soft living; neither will I consult the tastes and comforts of my spirit, in order that nothing may detain me in seeking my love on the toilsome mountains of virtue.'

The Gift of the Heart

As the hart wounded by a poisoned arrow cannot be easy and at rest but seeks relief from all sides, so the soul pierced by the arrow of love never ceases seeking to relieve its pains.

He who is in love is said to have lost his heart or to have had it stolen by the object of his love. His heart is not his own, but the property of the person he loves.

This consideration will enable the soul to discover whether it loves God simply or not. If it loves him it will have no heart for itself, nor for its own pleasure or profit, but for the honour, glory and pleasure of God; because the more the heart is occupied with itself, the less it is occupied with God. The soul can test itself by these signs: is it anxiously seeking God? Has it no pleasure in anything but him?

It is clear that the soul which loves God seeks no other reward for its services other than to love God perfectly.

On Death

Reveal your presence
And let the vision of your beauty kill
  me.
Behold, the malady
Of love is incurable
Except in your presence and before
  your face.

Death can hold no bitterness for the
soul that loves. It brings with it all the
sweetness and delights of love. There
is no sadness in the remembrance of it when it
opens the door to all joy. Nor can it be painful
and oppressive when it is the end of all unhappi-
ness and sorrow and the beginning of all good.
Yes, the soul looks upon it as a friend and bride,
and rejoices in thinking of it as the day of
espousals. It yearns for the day and hour of death
more than earthly kings long for principalities and
kingdoms.

True love accepts with perfect resignation, yes,
even with joy, whatever comes to it from the
hand of the Beloved, for 'perfect love casts out
fear'.

The Well

O crystal well!
O that on your silvered surface
You would mirror forth at once
Those eyes I have desired,
Which I bear sketched deep within my heart.

Faith is called crystal for two reasons: because it
is of Christ the Bridegroom, and because it has
the property of crystal, pure in its truth, a limpid
well without error or natural forms in it.

It is a well because the waters of spiritual goodness
flow from it to the soul. Christ our Lord speaking
to the Samaritan woman calls faith a well saying:
'The water that I shall give him will become in
him a well of water springing up to eternal life.'
This water is the Spirit, which those who believe
receive through faith in him.

I know the fountain well which flows and runs
    Though of the night.
That everlasting fountain is a secret well,
And I know well its home,
    Though of the night.
I know that nothing can be in beauty like it,
And that of it heaven and earth do drink,
    Though of the night.

The Approaches of Dawn

My beloved is the
   mountains,
The solitary wooded
   valleys,
The strange islands,
The raging torrents,
The whisper of the
   amorous breezes.

The tranquil night
At the approaches of dawn,
The silent music,
The murmuring solitude,
The supper which revives and enkindles love.

The divine light is here very appropriately called
the approaches of dawn, that is, the twilight. For
as the twilight of the morn disperses the light of
day, so the mind, tranquil and reposing in God,
is raised up from the darkness of natural knowledge to the morning light of the supernatural
knowledge of God.

Silent Music

In this silence and tranquillity of the night, and in this knowledge of the divine light, the soul discerns a marvellous arrangement and disposition of God's providence in the diversities of his creatures and operations. Each and all of them have a certain likeness to God, wherewith each, in its particular voice, tells of the God within it. This forms a concert of sublimest melody, far beyond all the harmonies of this world.

This is the silent music because it is knowledge, tranquil and calm, without audible voice; and thus the sweetness of music and the repose of silence are enjoyed in it.

The soul says that the Beloved is silent music because in him this harmony of spiritual music is understood and experienced.

As every one of the saints received the gifts of God in a different way, so every one of them sings his praises in a different way, and yet all harmonize in one concert of love.

The Sparrow

In contemplation the spirit has these five properties of the sparrow:

It generally frequents high places, and the spirit in this state rises to the highest contemplation.

It is ever turning its face in the direction of the wind, and the spirit turns its affections towards the place whence comes the spirit of love—God.

It is usually solitary, so the spirit in contemplation is far away from all worldly thoughts.

It sings most sweetly; and so does the spirit at this time sing to God. For the praises which it offers up spring from the sweetest love, delightful to itself and most precious in God's sight.

It is of no definite colour. So also is the perfect spirit which in this ecstasy is without any tinge of sensual affection or self-love. It has entered into the abyss of the knowledge of God.

Perfect Love

The more a soul loves, the more perfect it is in its love; hence it follows that the soul which is already perfect is, if we may speak in this manner, all love. All its actions are love, all its energies and strength are occupied in love. It gives up all it has like the wise merchant, for this treasure of love which it finds hidden in God.

The Beloved cares for nothing else but love. The soul therefore, anxious to please him perfectly, occupies itself unceasingly in pure love of God.

As the bee draws honey from all plants and makes use of them only for that end, so the soul most easily draws the sweetness of love from all that happens to it. It makes all things subservient to the end of loving God, whether they are sweet or bitter.

In all its occupations its joy is the love of God.

The Humility of God

God communicates himself to the soul in this interior union with a love so intense that the love of a mother who tenderly caresses her child, the love of a brother or the affection of a friend bears no resemblance to it.

Great is the tenderness and deep the love with which the Eternal Father comforts and exalts the loving soul.

O wonders worthy of awe and reverence! God humbles himself before the soul that he may exalt it, as if he were the servant and the soul his lord. He is as eager to comfort it as if he were a slave and the soul God, so great is the humility and tenderness of God.

In this communication of love he renders in a certain way those services to the soul which he says in the Gospel he will perform for the elect in heaven. 'Amen I say to you, he will gird himself and make them sit down to eat, and passing will minister to them.'

Loving Continually

My soul is occupied
And all my substance in his service.
Now I guard no flock,
Nor have I any other employment,
My sole occupation is love.

Before the soul succeeded in effecting this
gift and surrender of itself to the Beloved,
it was entangled in many useless occupations by which it sought to please itself
and others.

All this is over now, for all its thoughts, words
and actions are directed to God.

All my occupation now is the practice of the love
of God. All I do is done in love. All I suffer I
suffer in the sweetness of love. This is the meaning
of David when he says, 'I will keep my strength
to Thee.'

Singlemindedness

The soul, in the courage of its love, glories in what ministers to the Beloved, in that it has done anything for him, and is lost to the things of the world.

The soul remembers the words of the Bridegroom in the Gospel, 'No man can serve two masters', and therefore in order not to lose God, he loses all that is not God. He who truly loves makes shipwreck of himself in all else, that he may more easily gain the object of his love.

The soul loses itself, making no account whatever of itself but of the Beloved, resigning itself freely into his hands without any self-seeking. It holds everything of no value unless it serves the Beloved.

He that loves God seeks neither gain nor reward, but only to lose all, even himself.

Garlands of Beauty

Of emeralds and of flowers
In the early morning gathered,
We will make the garlands
Flowering in love,
And bound together with one hair of my head.

Good works wrought in the season of spiritual
dryness and hardness are like the freshness of the
winter morning. What we then do for God in
dryness of spirit is most precious in his eyes. It is
then that we acquire abundant virtues and graces,
and what we achieve with toil and labour is in
general better, more perfect and lasting than what
we acquire in spiritual sweetness.

All the virtues and graces which the soul, and
God within it, acquire, are like a wreath of divers
flowers, with which the soul is adorned as with a
richly embroidered cloak. Just as real flowers are
gathered and woven into a garland, so the spiritual
flowers are gathered and set in order in the soul.

The Dove

The little white dove
Has returned to the ark with
  the bough.
And now the turtle-dove
Its desired mate
On the green banks has found.

The Bridegroom calls the soul the turtle-dove because when it is seeking after the Beloved it is like the turtle-dove when it cannot find its desired mate. It is said that when it cannot find its mate it will not sit on any green bough, or drink cool refreshing water, nor rest in the shade, nor mingle with its companions. But when it finds its mate it does all these things.

Such too must be the soul if it is to attain union with the Bridegroom. The soul's love and anxiety must be such that it cannot rest on the green boughs of any joy, nor drink the waters of the world's honour and glory, nor recreate itself with any temporal comfort, nor shelter in the shade of created help and protection. It must mourn in its loneliness until it finds the Bridegroom to its heart's content.

The Blessings of Solitude

In solitude she lived
And in solitude built her nest;
And in solitude alone
Hath the Beloved guided her;
In solitude also wounded with love.

As the soul abode in solitude, abandoning all created help and consolation in order to obtain fellowship and union with the Beloved, it deserved thereby the peace of solitude in the Beloved, in whom it reposes alone, undisturbed by any anxiety.

The Bridegroom is also saying that, inasmuch as the soul has desired to be alone and far away from all created things, he has been enamoured of it because of its loneliness. He has taken care of it, held it in his arms, fed it with all good things and guided it to the depths of God.

The soul lived in solitude before it found the Beloved, for the soul that desires God receives no comfort from any other companion.

The Riches of Christ

There are in Christ great depths to be fathomed, for he is a rich mine with many recesses full of treasures. However deeply we may descend we shall never reach the end, for in every recess new veins of new treasure abound in every direction.

The soul cannot reach these hidden treasures unless it first passes through the thicket of interior and exterior sufferings. For even such knowledge of the mysteries of Christ as is possible in this life cannot be had without great suffering, and without many intellectual and moral gifts, and previous spiritual exercises. All these though are far inferior to the knowledge of the mysteries of Christ, and are merely a preparation for it.

The soul longs to enter in earnest into the caverns of Christ, that it may be absorbed, transformed and inebriated in the love and knowledge of his mysteries, hiding itself in the bosom of the Beloved. It is into these caverns that he invites the bride in the Canticle to enter saying: 'Arise my love, my fair one and come away, my dove in the cleft of the rock, in the coverts of the cliff.'

A New Springtime

The breathing of the air,
The song of the sweet nightingale,
The grove and its beauty
In the serene night,
With the flame that consumes and gives no pain.

As the song of the nightingale is heard in the
spring of the year, when the cold and rain and
changes of winter are past, filling the ear with
melody and the mind with joy; so in the true
intercourse and transformation of love which
takes place in this life the bride, now protected
and delivered from all trials and changes of the
world, detached and free from all the imperfections, sufferings and darkness both of mind and
body, becomes conscious of a new spring in
liberty, largeness and joy of spirit.

She hears the sweet voice of the Bridegroom, who
is her sweet nightingale, renewing and refreshing
the very substance of her soul, now prepared for
the journey of everlasting life.

Prayer of Trust

O sweetest love of God, too little
  known,
he who has found thee is at rest.
Let everything change O my God
that we may rest in thee.
Everywhere with thee O my
  God,
everywhere all things with thee
  as I wish.
O my God, all for thee, nothing for me.
Nothing for thee, everything for me.
All sweetness and delight for thee,
none for me.
All bitterness and trouble for me,
none for thee.
O my God how sweet to me thy presence
who art the sovereign good!
I will draw near to thee in silence
and will uncover thy feet,
that it may please thee to unite me with thyself
making my soul thy bride.
I will rejoice in nothing
till I am in thine arms.
O Lord, I beseech thee, leave me not for a
  moment
because I know not the value of my soul.

Afterword

JOHN'S MESSAGE FOR TODAY

We of the twentieth century are going back to the sources of Christianity. The Church no longer reigns triumphant; she is composed of the poor, the humble, the 'little ones' who must seek God in the silence and trust of pure faith—not looking for or wanting exterior proofs. In this, John of the Cross is a sure guide. He girds us for action, to *follow* Christ in faith by a complete self-denial. Do we not see in our modern psychology books the preoccupation with love, given and received? The man who wins through is the man who is able to forget self and want only the good of the Beloved. Love is proved by how we act towards the other, a readiness to bear, believe, hope, endure all things. Why should the relationship with God be different? John of the Cross is *not* the person to read if we are unwilling to *do* anything about love, and want merely to enjoy ephemeral (and basically selfish) dreams.

An old nun I knew had a favourite tale about a young woman, reclining on a well-cushioned sofa, beside her an open box of chocolates into which she dipped as she read the poetic stanzas of *The Spiritual Canticle*. 'Beautiful, beautiful', she sighed as she popped another chocolate into her mouth and snuggled down among the cushions! Yes, John can be read and enjoyed as a poet, but we misunderstand his imagery if we keep it at a superficial level; and he certainly will not allow this if we peruse his Commentaries as well as his lyrics.

John urges us forward when God seems 'absent', as he does to so many today when the comforting 'props' of a so-called Christian culture have been removed. Emotion passes, but true love is firm as a rock. The daily round faithfully accomplished, the inner battle to root out selfishness, the continual re-focusing on God as each duty presents itself, the desire to please him in all things; if we do this why search for visions and revelations, or inflamed emotions and sweet feelings? God is faithful. If we do what we can to the best of our ability he will complete the work himself.

Our scientific bent recognizes God's transcendence, so does John. There is no easy way by which God becomes a mere 'chum'. He remains God, we remain men, and we must see life in the light of this reality. All the demands of life are thus put in perspective. The Christian of today needs faith that the suffering he must undergo to uphold the values he believes in is ultimately worthwhile. Compromise is cowardice. Like the explorers of Everest, if we wish to ascend the mountain of Carmel to reach God, all else must be counted worthless, but at the summit we shall find the prize is Christ Jesus.

Index of Sources

Note on Translation and Selection

For the most part I have used as a guide David Lewis' translation of the works of St John of the Cross. However, as John's sentence structure is often involved and wordy I have in many cases simplified passages and telescoped sentences to a readable length. In this way I hope to reveal the kernel of John's teaching. There is likewise much Biblical imagery which I have omitted due to the fact that John's manner of using it is based on the scholastic expositions unfamiliar to most people today.

For those wishing to enjoy John's poetry I highly recommend the beautiful translation by Roy Campbell. A poet translating a poet has a unique capacity to capture the original.